RANDALL
the
Blue Spider
Goes Surfing

Written by
Ryeson & Shana Bull

Illustrated by
Brady Lovell

EAST 26TH
PUBLISHING

Randall the Blue Spider Goes Surfing
Copyright © 2021 by Shana Bull

Library of Congress Cataloging-in-Publication data is available
ISBN: 978-1-7348856-9-9

10 9 8 7 6 5 4 3 2 1
First printing edition 2021

East 26th Publishing
Houston, TX

Randall is a surfing spider.

He likes to visit the ocean and watch the waves crash.

The waves go crash and crash, over and over again.

Randall also loves to surf with his friend Chester the Caterpillar.

They spend hours and hours surfing in the water.

Randall wants to win the surfing competition.
He likes the nummy ice cream prize.

But Randall is also nervous.
There will be so many eyes watching him.

He's nervous about falling and getting laughed at.

Chester sees Randall hiding behind a palm tree and asks, "Why are you hiding?"

Randall says he's nervous that
everyone might laugh if he falls.

Chester has some advice for his friend.
"Everyone falls sometimes," he says. "Try rubbing your belly—
then you won't be nervous anymore!"

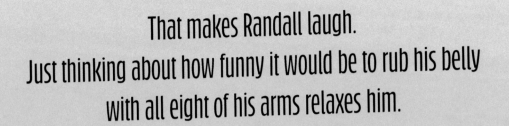

That makes Randall laugh.
Just thinking about how funny it would be to rub his belly
with all eight of his arms relaxes him.

So, Randall rubs his belly with all eight of his arms.

Then, he smiles, takes a deep breath, and goes to enter the surfing competition so he can win some ice cream.

When it is his turn to surf, Randall gets on his
surfboard and bravely rides a wave all the way to the shore.

Everybody claps and cheers for him.

Thanks to his friend Chester, who helped him face his fears, Randall wins second place in the surfing competition.

His prize is two ice creams.
Chester shared his advice with Randall, so
Randall shares his ice cream with Chester.

Because friends share.

THE
END

AUTHORS RYESON & SHANA BULL

By the time baby Ryeson Bull was smiling, he was telling stories with his actions. By age two he memorized *Goodnight Moon* and could repeat every line (yelling, of course). At age two-and-a-half, he dictated Randall the Blue Spider to his mama (co-author, Shana Bull) in a hospital parking lot in downtown Long Beach.

Ryeson was born with Cystic Fibrosis, a hereditary disease that impacts his lungs and digestive system. The ocean has always been a special place for the Bull family because salt air is good for Ryeson's lungs. Aside from the ocean, Rye loves reading, hiking, and playing outside with friends and random sticks he finds on the ground.

Ryeson's mama, Shana Bull, is a freelance writer and digital marketer with a focus on writing about travel, food, wine, music, and family life. Shana loves elaborate cheese boards, rosé wine, and adventures with her husband + Ryeson.

DISCOVER RANDALL & HIS FRIENDS
@randallthebluespider
randallthebluespider.com
hello@randallthebluespider.com